HEADSTART HISTORY PAPERS

Richard III

by

Keith Dockray

HEADSTART HISTORY

Published by Headstart History Publishing
        The History House, The Old Brewery
        Priory Lane, Burford,
        Oxon OX18 4SG GB

Printed by Parchment, Oxford

ISBN   1873041 81 0

A CIP catalogue record for this book is available at the British Library.

CONTENTS

Frontispiece: Richard III: artist unknown
                National Portrit Gallery

Many medieval English kings have bequeathed marvellous myths. King Alfred, when not carelessly burning the cakes, supposedly engaged in the happy tasks of fathering English unity, procreating the English navy and siring English prose. Ethelred II, in a befittingly casual fashion, soon earned his soubriquet the Unready. William of Normandy, by contrast, vigorously ensured that he would become known to history not as the Bastard but as the Conqueror. The first Richard worked assiduously at the task of becoming the Lionheart, leaving his younger brother John with only the negative option of inspiring Magna Carta. For Edward 1 there was the pressing need to win his reputation as the hammer of the Scots, while Edward II had to settle for giving the humble poker its one moment of notoriety in English history. And Henry V's destiny, of course, was to prove himself the arche-typal medieval English hero-king. History, it is clear, would be much the poorer without these - and so many other - splendid royal myths. Yet Richard III, arguably, has more claim to mythological distinction than any of them, since he has bequeathed not one enduring myth but two - as both an evil, murdering tyrant and an able, popular ruler.

1. An evil, murdering tyrant?

The first myth about Richard III - portraying him as a scheming, ruthless tyrant - not only developed early but also enjoyed the immense boost of receiving the blessing of England's greatest playwright, Shakespeare. In its fullest flowering, this has it that Richard, Duke of Gloucester (physically deformed and mentally warped as he was) set his sights on the throne as a young man; he eliminated, or connived at the elimination, of Henry VI, Henry VI's only son, Prince Edward of Lancaster and even his own brother George, Duke of Clarence, as a means of clearing the pathway to his own ambitions; and, once Edward IV was no more, he put his plans into action with a vengeance, cutting out the Woodvilles (the newly-widowed Queen Elizabeth and her family), seizing his nephews Edward V and Richard, Duke of York (and, in due course, securing their murder in the Tower of London), rigging the execution of William, Lord Hastings (the man most likely to stand in his way), and, within less than three months, acquiring the crown for himself. As king, he was unpopular from the start and, once the inevitably tyrannical nature of his rule fully revealed itself, he aroused such deep hostility and loathing in his oppressed people that they welcomed Henry Tudor, Earl of Richmond with open arms: Richard's own death at Bosworth and Henry VII's triumphant accession, indeed, provided an only too fitting denoument.

Even the king's contemporaries were frequently critical, most notably Dominic Mancini in his study of the usurpation of Richard III and the anonymous second continuator of the Crowland Chronicle. Mancini was an astute Italian commentator who was in England from the summer of 1482 until shortly after Richard III's coronation on 6 July 1483; he was writing very soon after the events he describes (his manuscript is dated 1 December

1483); and he was free from such political constraints as might have inhibited his English contemporaries. Moreover, although inclined to denigrate his own efforts, he seems, in fact, to have had good recall and, for the most part, presents an accurate account of events. His interpretation of what happened in the spring and early summer of 1483 is open to question. Seemingly, he was writing at the request of a patron and, perhaps, giving him the dramatic story he wanted; he may well have known no English; as a foreigner and outsider, his sources of information (hardly ever specified) may not have been all that reliable; and, puzzlingly, he provides no detailed pen portrait of Richard III (whereas he does supply such a picture of Edward IV). He tends to read back into Edward IV's reign tensions he observed only *after* the king's death and, as a source for the Woodvilles in particular, he must be treated with great caution: for instance, his suggestion that there was a long-standing jealousy between Richard of Gloucester and the queen's family may amount to no more than the retailing of anti-Woodville propaganda circulating in London. Also, he is clearly a hostile source for Richard III, presenting a subjective rather than objective view of events and, perhaps, reflecting here the sentiments of Edward V's supporters (the *losers* in 1483): certainly, he portrays Richard, in May and June 1483, as a master of dissimulation, motivated by intense ambition and an 'insane lust for power', ruthlessly removing men who stood in his way, and callously depriving his nephew of the throne so that he might take the crown for himself. 1

The second Crowland continuator is no less damning in his verdict on Richard III: indeed, his *personal* antagonism to the king and loathing of his entourage is only too evident. Although the identity of the chronicler is not known, he was clearly intelligent, a shrewd political observer and a man who was notably well-informed about many aspects of Yorkist politics and government. Yet, even more than Mancini, he presents a highly subjective - and notably hostile - interpretation of Richard III. Seemingly, he was a man who had served Edward IV for years and whose prime loyalty was to him and his sons: John Russell, Bishop of Lincoln, Richard Ill's chancellor for most of his reign, might fit the bill but, if so, it is strange that his knowledge of 1483-1485 appears so much less sure than his coverage of the 1470s. More promising, perhaps, is a recently retired chancery official Henry Sharp. If the author of the Crowland Chronicle was, indeed, an elderly cleric whose memory had seen better days, by April 1486 (when he probably set pen to paper), this would at least explain the falling off in quality the source. What is highly probable is that the chronicler's customary anti-northern stance, as well as several months of pro-Tudor propaganda, coloured his treatment of Richard of Gloucester's career throughout. Even before 1483, he comments adversely on Richard's conduct during an expedition to Scotland in 1482 and, although he had no great enthusiasm for the Woodvilles, he firmly disapproved of the Protector's execution of William, Lord Hastings, regarded his northern connection as alien and undesirable, and condemned his arbitrary seizure of the throne; his treatment of the king's reign is generally hostile as well, not least his scathing comments on Richard III's behaviour in connection with the illness and death of his wife (early in 1485), his excessive financial exactions and, most of all, the tyrannical northern-dominated regime which, he believed, Richard established in southern England. Nevertheless, his is the most important description we have of Richard of Gloucester's protectorate, usurpation and short reign as king. **2**

The work of both Mancini and the second Crowland continuator certainly indicates that there was a substantial foundation of southern hostility to Richard III - pre-dating his defeat and death at Bosworth - on which Tudor writers were able to build with devastating results. During the reigns of the first two Tudor kings, in fact, there developed a powerful tradition of the Tudor dynasty as the saviour of England from the chaos and confusion of the Wars of the Roses. Neither Henry VII nor Henry VIII seem to have had a deliberate policy often mounting a full-scale campaign against Richard III designed to blacken his name: nevertheless, 1485 did tend to be portrayed by Polydore Vergil, Edward Hall and their successors as a turning-point in English history, with Henry VII cast as the inaugurator of a 'brave new world' and Richard III (as Henry's immediate predecessor and the king whom he defeated at the battle of Bosworth) the victim of ever-increasing denigration. Even the Crowland chronicler, as early as April 1486, firmly took on board the already current notion of Henry VII as a dynastic peacemaker. The Warwickshire antiquary John Rous, in his *History of the Kings of England* (written shortly before his death in 1491), penned a vociferously hostile portrait of the king as the unnatural product of two years in his mother's womb, 'emerging with teeth and hair to his shoulders', a man who, 'like a scorpion, combined a smooth front and a stinging tail', and a king who ruled 'in the way that Antichrist is to reign'. **3** Similarly, *London Chronicles* put together in early Tudor times seem only too willing to criticise Richard III and take on board rumours circulating about him: the *Great Chronicle of London*, for instance, concluded that the king died 'with dishonour as he that sought it' and, as a result, 'now his fame is decried and dishonoured'.**4**

No early Tudor sources have been more influential in promulgating the Black Legend about Richard III than Polydore Vergil and Sir Thomas More. The Italian scholar and fully-fledged Renaissance historian Polydore Vergil was already at work on his *English History* before the death of the first Tudor king in 1509. He consulted many men who could remember well back into the Yorkist period; he showed himself nicely aware of conflicting interpretations; he genuinely attempted to distinguish fact from fiction; and he firmly sought to establish the relationship between cause and effect. Additionally, he had access to a range of written materials (including one or more London chronicles and, perhaps, the text of the second Crowland continuator). Nevertheless, he was encouraged to write a history of England by his patron Henry VII; he dedicated the completed work to Henry VIII; and his treatment of Richard III clearly reflects the sources available to him (almost all hostile to the king). Although no official hack and prepared to admit that Richard III had some good qualities (notably courage), Vergil must certainly be regarded as one of the major architects of later Tudor tradition about the last Plantagenet king. As soon as he heard of Edward IV's death, Vergil tells us, Richard 'began to be kindled with an ardent desire of sovereignty' and determined thereafter 'to accomplish his purposed spiteful practice by subtlety and sleight'; subsequently, 'being blind with covetousness of reigning, whom no foul fact could now hold back', he seized the throne 'without assent of the commonalty' and did so 'contrary to the law of God and man'; and, given the fact that Richard 'thought of nothing but tyranny and cruelty', at the finish God gave victory at Bosworth to Henry VII. **5**

Undoubtedly, the most influential early Tudor writer on Richard III was Sir Thomas More. His *History of King Richard III*, written (in English and Latin concurrently) in the early part of Henry VIII's reign but mysteriously abandoned unfinished and unrevised by its author, was not, in fact, published until after More's death; he may not have seen himself as writing history at all; he is frequently inaccurate, often prepared to embellish his narrative for dramatic effect, and primarily concerned to portray Richard as a great villain and a usurping tyrant. Yet More did have access to earlier written sources; he was not writing to please any particular patron; and he did, on occasion, attempt to distinguish between rumour and fact. A strong case can be made, indeed, for saying that More's basic characterisations and story-line already mapped out to a significant extent in earlier (including contemporary) narratives - are not only plausible but even convincing. Certainly, he provides far more detail than Vergil on Richard III's character, behaviour and the sequence of events from April to October 1483. Here, for instance, is More's famous description of Richard's deformities:

...little of stature, ill-featured of limbs, crookbacked, his left shoulder much higher than his right, hard-favoured of visage...He was malicious, wrathful, envious and, from before his birth, ever forward. It is for truth reported that the duchess his mother had so much ado in her labour that she could not be delivered of him uncut, and that he came into the world with the feet forward [and] also not untoothed.

Moreover, according to More, he 'spared no man's death whose life withstood his purpose'. **6**

Later Tudor sources, notably Edward Hall and Raphael Holinshed, derived most of their information from Polydore Vergil and Sir Thomas

More. Edward Hall, however, both added to and deepened the hostile portrait bequeathed to him, and his Richard III, an out-and-out monster and tyrant, fully deserved his fate at the hands of that agent of divine providence Henry VII. The Elizabethan chroniclers Grafton and Holinshed took over Hall's interpretation virtually in its entirety: Holinshed, indeed, only rarely rises above the level of plagiarism, happily lifting great chunks from the earlier works of More and Hall and incorporating them into his narrative. William Shakespeare, seemingly, read both Hall and Holinshed, and his gripping play Richard III (put together in the early 1590s) represents the magnificent dramatic climax of almost a century of ever-growing denigration. Here we find Richard III as the fully-fledged personification of evil, an ambitious monster unable to share in idle pleasures on account of his deformity, and a man who takes a positive delight in his own wickedness: indeed, it is the fact that Richard is not only evil but witty with it which makes Shakespeare's portrayal so devastating. And, since the play has continued to be read and performed regularly over the centuries, Shakespeare has inadvertently ensured that Tudor tradition and the popular view of Richard III have remained virtually synonymous.7

Certainly, Tudor portrayals exercised a powerful influence in the seventeenth and eighteenth centuries: Sir Walter Raleigh, in 1614, dismissed him as 'the greatest monster in mischief of all that forwent him'; Francis Bacon, in 1621, believed he was exceptionally prone to ambition, deceit and even wickedness; and in 1762 over a century later, David Hume concluded that Richard was 'hump-backed and had a very disagreeable visage': his body, moreover, was 'in every particular no less deformed than his mind'. In 1819 the Roman Catholic John Lingard condemned 'that monster in human shape, Richard III' as 'a prince of insatiable ambition who could conceal the most bloody projects under the mask of affection and loyalty'; In 1874 J.R. Green pictured the king as ambitious, ruthless, pitiless and, when he deemed it necessary, prepared to throw off any pretence of constitutional rule; and Bishop William Stubbs adopted a tone of deep disapproval in his *Constitutional History of England,* concluding that Richard was cunning, unscrupulous and 'amenable to no instincts of mercy or kindness'.8 Richard III's Victorian biographer James Gairdner did not like him much either. The 'scantiness of contemporary evidence and the prejudices of original authorities,' Gairdner declared in 1878:

... can hardly be expected to weaken the conviction - derived from Shakespeare and tradition as much as from anything else - that Richard was indeed cruel and unnatural beyond the ordinary measure even of those violent and ferocious times.9

And critical, even intemperate, verdicts on Richard III have continued to be returned in the twentieth century. Indeed, A.L. Rowse, in a dreadful book entitled *Bosworth Field and the Wars of the Roses* (published in 1966), took on board Tudor tradition more or less in its entirety, comparing Richard with Adolf Hitler, and finding highly questionable parallels between Richard's government and that prevailing in Germany under Nazi rule! **10** No less strikingly, in 1983, Desmond Seward published what he himself described as 'the most hostile life of Richard III to appear for over a century', concluding that the king:...possessed the qualities of an Italian tyrant. He was the most terrifying man ever to occupy the English throne. **11**

2. An able, popular ruler?

The second myth about Richard III - suggesting that, but for his tragic death at Bosworth in August 1485, he might well have gone down in history as a most accomplished and successful king - can also be traced back to contemporary sources. Such a portrayal has it that, as Duke of Gloucester, Richard had been a loyal servant of his brother, an able ruler of the north and a successful soldier. His seizure of the throne, although dramatic and unexpected, was nevertheless justified in that it saved England from the horrors of a Woodville-dominated regime and preserved Richard himself from being unjustly humiliated. And, although he ruled for just two years, the quality of his government - particularly his zeal for impartial justice and concern for the well-being of ordinary folk - was only too apparent. To some extent such a favourable image resulted from the king's own propaganda. The 1484 statute settling the crown on Richard III and his descendants, for instance, incorporated what purported to be a petition presented to him in June 1483, urging him to take the throne as a man of exemplary character devoted to good government and 'naturally inclined to the prosperity and common weal' of the realm. Nor can Thomas Langton Bishop of St. David's be regarded as impartial: a northerner from Appleby in Westmorland, he was appointed to the Bishopric of St. David's during Richard's protectorate (in May 1483) and, in February 1485, rewarded with Lionel Woodville's former and much richer see of Salisbury. Yet it is surely significant that, when writing to his friend and fellow humanist William Selling, Prior of Christ Church, Canterbury, in August 1483, he declared that the king:

...contents the people wherever he goes better than ever did any prince; for many a poor man that has suffered wrong many days has been relieved and helped by him and his commands in his progress. And in many great cities and towns were great sums of money given to him which he has refused. On my faith I never liked the qualities of any prince as well as his; God has sent him to us for the welfare of us all.

The Warwick chaplain John Rous, in the so-called Rous Roll (a history of the Earls of Warwick) written during Richard III's reign, praised the king in notably extravagant terms:

The most mighty Prince Richard...all avarice set aside ruled his subjects in his realm full commendably, punishing offenders of his laws, especially extortioners and oppressors of his commons, and cherishing those that were virtuous, by which discreet guiding he got great thanks of God and love of all his subjects, rich and poor, and great praise of the people of all other lands about him. **12**

Even in his generally hostile *History of the Kings of England*, written early in the reign of Henry VII, Rous commended Richard as a builder and a patron, a man who, early in his reign, refused offers of money from London, Gloucester and Worcester, 'affirming that he would rather have their love than their treasure', and a king who, on the battlefield at Bosworth, 'bore himself like a gallant knight [and] honourably defended himself to his last breath'. Dominic Mancini, while notably critical of Richard's behaviour in 1483, nevertheless recorded that in the last years of Edward IV's reign:

The good reputation of his private life and public activities powerfully attracted the esteem of strangers. Such was his renown in warfare that, whenever a difficult and dangerous policy had to be undertaken, it would be entrusted to his discretion and generalship. By these skills Richard acquired the favour of the people...

A Scottish envoy Archibald Whitelaw, in an oration to Richard during an audience in 1484, declared that he was a king of great spirit, while a visiting Italian humanist, Pietro Carmeliano (who, after he had entered the service of Henry VII, was to condemn Richard III as the villainous murderer of Henry VI and the Princes in the Tower!) reported in the same year:

If we look [for] religious devotion, what prince is there in our time who shows a more genuine piety? If for justice, who can we reckon above him throughout the world? If we look for prudence in fostering peace and waging war, who shall we judge his equal? If we look for truth of soul, for wisdom, for loftiness of mind united with modesty, who stands before our King Richard? What Christian Emperor or Prince can be compared with him in good works and munificence? To whom are theft, rebellion, pollution, adultery, manslaughter, usury, heresy and other abominable crimes more hateful than to him? Obviously, no one.

And, when news of Bosworth reached the city, it was put on record in York that Richard had been 'piteously slain and murdered, to the great heaviness of this city'. Even hostile Tudor commentators had the occasional word of commendation. Polydore Vergil, for instance, allowed that Richard's courage:...*high and fierce...failed him not in the very death [when] he rather yielded to be taken with the sword than by foul flight prolong his life...* William Camden, in his monumental *Brittania* (published in 1586), while recording that Richard 'inhumanly murdered his nephews' and usurped the throne, nevertheless reported that 'in the opinion of the wise he is reckoned in the number of bad men but of good princes'; Camden's contemporary John Stow, even more positively, remarked that not only was Richard's responsibility for the murder of his nephews unproven but also that old men (who had seen the king) had told him that, although low in stature, he was not deformed; and, towards the end of Elizabeth's reign, there was already circulating Sir William Cornwallis's *Brief Discourse in Praise of King Richard the Third* (although, in fact, this seems to have been merely a rhetorical exercise in defence of the indefensible!)

The first full-scale defence of Richard III came from the pen of Sir George Buck, Master of the Revels to James I, in the early seventeenth century. Convinced that 'all King Richard's guilt is but suspicion' and determined 'to rescue him entirely from these wrongs'. Buck, a conscientious antiquarian-cum-historian who consulted a range of manuscripts (including the second continuation of the Crowland Chronicle), produced the first comprehensive assault on Tudor tradition and concluded that the king's 'good name and noble memory' had, indeed, been foully maligned. Certainly, Buck not only praised Richard's courage, fortitude, magnanimity, justice and piety but also pointed out that: ...*even his adversaries and calumniators confess that he was a very wise and a prudent and politic and an heroical prince...*13 William Winstanley, in 1684, found Richard III 'a man of admirable parts'; Rapin, in the early eighteenth century, considered him a basically good man sadly corrupted by ambition; and Horace Walpole, in his classic defence of the king (first published in 1767), concluded that many of the crimes attributed to Richard were not only improbable but clearly at odds with both his character and his own interests.14 Caroline Halsted, in 1844, was even more outspoken, commenting warmly on his 'shining abilities, his cultivated mind, his legislative wisdom, his generosity [and] his clemency', and concluding that "...among all the heavy and fearful charges brought against him, few, if any, originate with his contemporaries." 15 In 1906 came Sir Clements Markham's colourful biography of the king where the real Richard III, properly rescued from *the accumulated garbage and filth of centuries of calumny*, turns out to be one of the best kings England has ever had. Philip Lindsay, in 1933, was no less enthusiastic:

...destiny could not break [Richard's] spirit, the spirit that is England. Nothing could destroy that spark that Richard carried in his breast, the spirit

that kept him fighting, struggling on, when he could see nothing but blackness ahead. Indomitable, heroic and lovable, the great Richard, last of our English kings.

Favourable too, although both more scholarly and better researched, was Paul Murray Kendall's popular biography of 1955. In the course of 'a mere eighteen months crowded with cares and problems', Kendall concluded, Richard III: *...laid down a coherent programme of legal enactments, maintained an orderly society and actively promoted the well-being off his subjects...***16**

Even Charles Ross's frequently critical 1981 biography of the king firmly rejected the monster and villain of Tudor tradition.

3. The recent debate
Charles Ross's authoritative study must now provide the foundation for anyone wishing to embark on the serious study of Richard III. His Richard was, in many respects, a strikingly conventional later medieval prince, but he was also very much a product of the violent and ruthless era of the Wars of the Roses. He shared to the full the delight off his age in luxury and display; his court was lively and impressive; and he was an enthusiastic patron of building. Professing a piety that was as sincere as it was considerable, he made a number of religious foundations, promoted learned men to high ecclesiastical office and proved himself a firm protector of the church. Yet his *political* behaviour certainly left much to be desired. He employed character-assassination as a deliberate instrument of policy; he frequently and violently denounced his enemies (especially the Woodvilles andTudor partisans) for their vices and debauchery; and he publicly humiliated his brother's former mistress Elizabeth ('Jane') Shore. His seizure of the crown in June 1483 was in fact, and was widely seen to be at the time, 'an unashamed bid for personal power': the political nation in general had no desire to see young Edward V removed from the throne, still less murdered in the Tower of London (that Edward V and his brother were indeed murdered, and in 1483, and on Richard III's orders, Ross considered highly likely). The cardinal fact in Richard's reign, he argued, was the urgent need to attract support, for never had a king' usurped the throne with so narrow a basis of support from the nobility as a whole or with so little popular enthusiasm'. Richard III, indeed, was dangerously dependent on his *northern* connection; Buckingham's rebellion demonstrated only too clearly the degree of resentment and distrust of his regime felt throughout the *southern* counties of the realm; and, after its collapse, the need to win enhanced backing assumed the character of a race against time. Certainly, he did make an all out effort to secure committed support, particularly among the nobility, and he enjoyed considerable success in this (as is shown

by the impressive turn-out for him at Bosworth). An ambitious and ruthless politician he undoubtedly was, but he was also an effective political operator who, having usurped the throne, disposed of his nephews and crushed a major rebellion, perhaps came nearer than is often allowed to establishing himself and his northern connection permanently in the corridors and places of power in fifteenth-century England. 17

It is now almost twenty years now since Ross's biography was published and, during the intervening decade, there has been no sign of any lessening of interest in the king. On the contrary, books and articles have continued to roll off the presses, most notably from the pens of Colin Richmond, Charles Wood, Rosemary Horrox, Michael Hicks and A.J.Pollard. All, in various ways and to varying degrees, have been critical of Richard III. Among them, Charles Wood is exceptional in his firm rejection of the notion that Richard of Gloucester, in the months following Edward IV's death, proved himself a calculating politician who systematically pursued his own perceived self-interest. Rather, he has portrayed Richard as a man notably lacking in political foresight, ever moving from 'one unexpected crisis to the next', and following a notably 'blundering path' to regality. For several weeks in the spring of 1483 his goals seem to have been distinctly limited as he strove to keep his options open, but he did have every reason to fear the Woodvilles and his legitimate expectation of an enduring high-profile political role as Edward V's uncle was by no means assured. Before the seizure and execution of William, Lord Hastings on 13 June 1483, however, there is little evidence that Richard had decided to depose his nephew; rather, despite his tactical skill in gaining custody of Edward V at Stony Stratford on 30 April:

...nothing in the record of the next month and a half suggests a man of much political finesse or sagacity. Far from dominating the situation, Richard appears to have been trapped by it, uncertain what his next move should be. [Each] option appears to have been grasped on the spur of the moment, with inadequate regard for its effectiveness or likely political consequences. These were the actions more of a foolish man than a calculating one.

Perhaps the discovery that Hastings was involved in a conspiracy against him finally triggered Richard's regal ambitions but, even in the days that followed, there was a good deal of uncertainty and confusion (for instance, regarding the grounds on which he might most convincingly claim the throne) until, at last, he became King Richard III on 26 June. Nor did his political acumen develop notably over the next two years: during his early weeks on the throne he lived in a fool's paradise; the rebellions of October 1483 took him completely by surprise; and, in 1485, he had no choice but to abandon the foolish project of marrying his own niece. On the battlefield of Bosworth, moreover, Richard:

...died very much as he had lived: blindly unrepentant, fittingly unshriven, and in a characteristically dramatic charge. It was but the last of his bold and impetuous gambles, a desperate attempt to win back a kingdom that he knew was on the verge of being lost. **18**

Colin Richmond has no time for the notion of Richard III as an incompetent blunderer in 1483, reacting to events rather than controlling them, but he *is* firmly wedded to the traditional portrayal of the king as '*the* wicked uncle' whose sheer audacity 'left experienced politicians gasping'. At Stony Stratford on 30 April he took Anthony Woodville, Earl Rivers 'entirely by surprise'; William, Lord Hastings, on 13 June, was likewise taken completely unawares; and Richard's usurpation, a few days later, came as a shock to everyone. As for the much-rumoured fate of the Princes in the Tower, it played a major role in bringing about the king's well-deserved defeat and death at Bosworth:

Unconventional as Richard's moves were in the usurpation, which was for that very reason successful as conventional politicians were swept aside in stunned disbelief, the culminating and most unconventional of the series (the disappearance of the Princes in the Tower) had repercussions far beyond the political world in Westminster and the home counties. Although Richard, when he put down the rising of October 1483, may have thought that world had been conquered, it was the wider one of English provincial politics which, so to speak, conquered him at Bosworth. Even the lukewarmness of his northerners, manifest at Bosworth, may have had its origin in what he had done or was held to have done to the Princes. **19**

In 1989 Rosemary Horrox deliberately eschewed matters like Richard III's personality and the fate of his nephews - which have so often formed the enigmatic battleground between the king's denigrators and defenders.Instead, she concentrated her attention on royal patronage and the role of the king's servants during the turbulent years of his high-profile career. As Duke of Gloucester, she concluded, Richard proved himself 'the effective and trusted servant of his brother Edward IV circa 1471 to 1483 and *their relationship is a copy-book example of the mutual advantages of good lordship*: his rule of the north during these years was notably successful, he built up a powerful affinity there, and his loyalty to the crown was beyond reproach. Yet his interests were never exclusively northern and, as constable and admiral of England, he was consistently active on the national stage. When he seized the throne in 1483 he did so not from outside the prevailing political structure but from its heart and what is most notable about this protectorate and early months as king was the degree of *continuity* with his brother's regime. Of course he was ambitious, obviously enjoyed the exercise of power, chose to dictate events following his brother's death, and eventually took the crown in late June 1483 (even though the protectorate was still viable): indeed, he engineered his progress to the throne by a series of pre-emptive strikes which shook the Yorkist establishment to its very foundations and rendered it powerless to resist him. The critical turning-point in his fortunes, however, was Buckingham's rebellion in the autumn of 1483, when his brother's men deserted him in droves and Henry Tudor, Earl of Richmond first emerged as a serious rival. The continuity of service was now irrevocably broken and he had no choice but to reassert royal authority virtually from scratch. Moreover, although the king made very considerable efforts to widen the basis of his support in 1484/5 (and never *swamped* the south of England with northerners), he was forced, in practice, more and more into dependence on his still overwhelmingly north-country affinity. Consequently, at Bosworth (a battle which 'should have been fought in October 1483' he was backed very largely by the same men who had brought him to power. He certainly needed a decisive victory but, while coming very close to success, he failed in the end, and his own death on the field made the accession of Henry VII inevitable. Richard III 'destroyed the house of York', Horrox concluded, and he also 'destroyed himself' : the Tudor chronicler Edward Hall was 'surely right to see his reign as a tragedy'.**20**

Two years after the appearance of Rosemary Horrox's fine monograph, Michael Hicks published a characteristically provocative study of *Richard III. The Man Behind the Myth*. He judged the king to be an able, intelligent, well-organised man, a natural leader who was loyal and generous to his retainers as well as possessing a good deal of personal charm, and a well-read, sincerely religious patron of learning and the church. Neither a cripple nor incapable of bearing arms, he could, when it suited him, prove single-mindedly ambitious, aggressive and ruthless; he was not a great general (the 1482 expedition to Scotland, on which his military reputation largely rests, was deliberately projected as a triumph by Gloucester *himself,* and the second Crowland continuator, for one, did not believe it) nor a chivalric hero; nor was he, by nature, a peacemaker or even a genuine man of the north. Until his brother Edward IV's death he pursued a career of continuous and conspicuous service to the crown both on the national stage and in the north of England (where, increasingly, he came to see his future and where, certainly, he had achieved a notably dominant position by April 1483, albeit as a result of 'a judicious mixture of violence, chicanery and self-publicity'). His usurpation, the product of three months of calculated scheming and dissimulation (when he, first, systematically cut the ground from beneath his opponents' feet, and then, while the Yorkist establishment was still reeling, moved to press home his advantage by taking the throne itself), resulted not from principle or concern for the common weal but perceived personal advantage: Richard may have believed his own propaganda that he was indeed the man best suited to rule England but it is doubtful if his behaviour aroused much enthusiasm in the political nation. During his early months as king he worked very hard, seemingly, to persuade people - especially his brother's former men - that his kingship was legitimate, projecting a notably positive image of himself as the very model of a just ruler. Buckingham's rebellion demonstrated the extent of his failure when virtually the whole Yorkist establishment in southern England, deeply hostile to his regime as it was, rose in arms against him. Moreover, although the king was able to contain the insurrection, many rebels fled abroad, many more only reluctantly made their peace (and remained dissatisfied), and, ominously, Henry Tudor had now emerged as a new focus for opposition. Richard III, forced to rely increasingly on his own personal affinity, exposed himself to charges of tyranny as a result; his enemies, in 1484-5, mounted a vigorous campaign of vilification against him; and his defeat and death at Bosworth appeared to justify all their vociferous criticisms. **21**

A.J. Pollard, a seasoned campaigner in the Ricardian wars, published his perceptive, entertaining and superbly illustrated *Richard III and the Princes in the Tower* at about the same time as Michael Hicks's rival offering. The inner man, he concluded, must remain as enigmatic and elusive as ever. Even if, outwardly, Richard appears able, intelligent, self-confident (at any rate until the last months of his life), brave, chivalrous, generous, just and pious. There is no less a body of evidence showing him as a ruthless master of political intrigue and chicanery where his own personal ambitions and objectives were concerned. Until 1483 he was unswervingly loyal to Edward IV and, during the 1470s, he became both a great national figure and a powerful northern lord: indeed, in the north of England, he put an end to the civil strife that had plagued the region since 1453, actively promoted impartial justice and, by his victorious (and, among northerners, popular) campaign against the Scots in 1482, earned himself a formidable military reputation. Although there are no reliable indications that Richard entertained regal ambitions before 1483 and, even thereafter, it is not clear just when he set his sights on the throne, he certainly never surrendered the initiative once he had seized Edward V at Stony Stratford on 30 April. Indeed, he very much dictated events, acted with a decisiveness and ruthlessness that completely wrong-footed his rivals, and made himself king at the end of June to the amazement of contemporaries and stunned paralysis of the Yorkist establishment. Yet his political judgement in taking the throne, an act that, in the end, led to his destruction rather than his preservation, is questionable; so too is the elimination of his nephews (whose murder he probably ordered before mid-September 1483), since rumours of their fate outraged many of his subjects and, no doubt, helped make them even less willing to accept him as king. Moreover, although largely restricted to southern counties from Essex to Cornwall (the north and midlands stood by the king) and poorly coordinated, Buckingham's rebellion was a serious affair. In its aftermath Richard certainly needed to destroy the makeshift alliance of Edwardian Yorkists and diehard Lancastrians who had backed it, secure the dissident south and eliminate the Tudor threat. Even the limited success of his early efforts, however, had a hollow ring to it and, as time passed, the king found himself having to rely ever more overtly on those whom he believed he could best trust (particularly members of his northern affinity); his credibility problem remained obstinately resistant to enduring solution; and, as the self-confidence he had exuded in 1483 evaporated, he may well have begun to crack under the strain during his last months. Finally, in August 1485, his own reckless behaviour in the field at Bosworth (a battle he should have won since he outnumbered his enemies and probably had the advantage of the terrain) brought not only his own death but also the downfall of the Yorkist dynasty.22

4. Neither Monster nor Mogul?

Richard III's personality remains as enigmatic as ever and his behaviour open to more than one interpretation. Evidently his reputation has indeed suffered at the hands of critical southern-orientated chroniclers at the time, hostile London commentators both before and after 1485, and, most of all, evolving Tudor tradition during the sixteenth century: it is certainly unfortunate that there exists no contemporary or near-contemporary *northern* chronicle since, if there did, it might well present a very different picture of him. Nevertheless, historians must do the best they can with the evidence that is available.

Certainly, the deformed Tudor monster can safely be rejected: Shakespeare's 'bottled spider' has no justification in reality. True, as early as May 1491, we have the intriguing report (in the records of the city of York) of an unseemly incident during which William Burton of York, a drunken schoolmaster, declared that 'King Richard was a hypocrite, a crook back [and] was buried in a dyke like a dog', while John Rous, at about the same time, remarked on his uneven shoulders: *contemporary* sources, however, are entirely silent on the matter. Nicholas von Poppelau, a Bohemian knight who met the king in May 1484, reported that Richard was 'three fingers taller than myself, also much slimmer', and had 'delicate arms and legs' (an enigmatic description if ever there was one!). A Scottish envoy Archibald Whitelaw, also in 1484, declared that never had so much spirit reigned in so small a body. Neither Whitelaw nor von Poppelau, interestingly, suggest any physical deformity, if any deformity at all. Nor, for that matter, do early portraits of Richard III: the portrait of the king in Windsor castle, for instance, painted some thirty years after Richard's death (although probably based on a more nearly contemporary likeness) owes its deformed shoulder only to later alteration (as X-ray examination has made clear). In all probability, the Tudor hunchback does derive from some oddity about Richard III - but it might be no more than the fact that he seems to have been significantly shorter than his two brothers.

The riddle of Richard III's personality cannot, in the last analysis, be resolved. Clearly, he did not share Edward IV's uninhibited love of pleasure (although he did sire at least one, possibly two, bastards); there is some evidence that his marriage of convenience to Anne Neville was not, on that account, entirely barren of affection; and, certainly, the death of his only son in 1484 appears to have caused him real distress. As A.J. Pollard has recently remarked, we can surely observe in Richard 'a personal, knowledgeable and sincere piety': yet it is no less evident that he also had some of the less endearing characteristics of an early modern Puritan or even a present day born-again Christian. His vituperative condemnation of the morals of his opponents in general, and his humiliation of Edward IV's former courtesan Mistress Shore in particular, leave a nasty taste in the mouth, and it is difficult to avoid the conclusion, given his own amoral (if not immoral) behaviour on occasion, that there was a streak of hypocrisy in him - as, indeed, there was a capacity for self-deception and a tendency to swallow his own hyperbolical propaganda. A capable military commander (as he demonstrated during the expedition to Scotland in 1482), there seems little doubt either that he was personally courageous (as his behaviour on the battlefield of Bosworth shows). As an administrator, too, he was not without ability (as his record both in the north of England and, later, as king amply displays). Moreover, he possessed a real capacity to inspire loyalty (as best shown by the firm backing he generally received from his powerful northern connection). Yet, equally clearly, he was inordinately ambitious for power, ruthless in his pursuit of it (even if this involved dissimulation and deception) and capable not only of contemplating but also sanctioning the removal of men (or children!) who stood in his way.

Born at Fotheringhay in Northamptonshire in 1452, Richard seems to have enjoyed a conventional aristocratic upbringing; exiled for several months following the death of his father at the battle of Wakefield on 30 December 1460, he returned to England in time to participate in his brother Edward IV's coronation on 28 June 1461 (when, despite his extreme youth, he was accorded the highest respect and deference); and, in the autumn of 1461, he was raised to the dukedom of Gloucester. During the later 1460s he spent several years in Warwick the Kingmaker's household (when, it is reasonable to assume, he developed a considerable affection for Warwick's Yorkshire castle of Middleham and its surrounding countryside, which he retained for the rest of his life); early in 1469 he was recalled to the royal court by Edward IV and, a few months later, created Constable of England (at the age of seventeen); and, during the crisis of 1469 to 1471 when Warwick challenged the Yorkist king's authority, he proved notably loyal to his brother. Richard of Gloucester fled to Burgundy with Edward in the autumn of 1470; he shared his months in exile there and returned with him to England in the spring of 1471; and he played a prominent part in the battles of Barnet and Tewkesbury (which firmly re-established Edward IV on the throne). Indeed, Gloucester's alleged involvement in the murder of Prince Edward of Lancaster following Tewkesbury was eventually to figure as the first major incident in later Tudor denigration of Richard (although, in fact, the prince was almost certainly slain during the battle itself). There is a stronger case for Richard of Gloucester's participation in the murder of Henry VI in the Tower of London shortly after: the balance of likelihood, however, is that Edward IV himself was responsible for Henry's death (with Gloucester either playing no part at all or, at most, acting in a supervisory capacity on his brother's behalf).

Certainly, Richard of Gloucester's behaviour during the crisis of 1469 to 1471 was in marked contrast to that of his other surviving brother George, Duke of Clarence. In the later 1460s Clarence had fallen under the spell of Warwick the Kingmaker, married his daughter Isabel and backed the Readeption of Henry VI in the autumn of 1470. No doubt dissatisfied at his treatment thereafter, he was reconciled with Edward IV (in April 1471) and, after Warwick's death at Barnet and Edward's restoration, clearly anticipated great rewards (not least from the Warwick inheritance). Gloucester, meanwhile, determined to marry the Kingmaker's younger daughter Anne, himself, and the result of this, and the desire of both to reap maximum profit from royal patronage, was a great quarrel between the two brothers lasting well over two years. Gloucester did, in fact, marry Anne Neville; both he and Clarence benefited considerably from Edward's generosity; and the king eventually managed to engineer a reconciliation between his brothers (albeit at the expense of both Warwick's widow, the Dowager Countess Anne, and her six year old nephew George Neville.). Within a few years, however, Clarence had been arrested and committed to the Tower (in July 1477), and, a few months after that, following a form of trial in parliament, he met a violent death (perhaps by drowning in a butt of malmsey wine). Dominic Mancini, perhaps reflecting anti-Woodville propaganda disseminated by Richard of Gloucester in 1483, suggests that Queen Elizabeth Woodville engineered Clarence's fall while Gloucester was overcome with grief at his brother's death. Sir Thomas More, by contrast, reports the belief 'of some wise men' in the early sixteenth century that:

[Gloucester's] drift, covertly conveyed, lacked not in helping forth his brother Clarence to his death, which he resisted openly, howbeit somewhat, as men deemed, more faintly than he that were heartily minded to his welfare.

Certainly, it is interesting that the queen backed Gloucester against Clarence over the Warwick inheritance in the early 1470s; Gloucester, seemingly, attended the crucial planning meetings in late 1477 and helped pack the parliament that condemned his brother; and he benefited more than anyone else from Clarence's demise. Nevertheless, as the well-informed second Crowland continuator makes clear, it was, in fact, Edward IV *himself* who played the pivotal role in bringing about Clarence's disgrace and death.

The Tudor chronicler Edward Hall believed that Richard III 'more loved, more esteemed and regarded the northern men than any subjects within his realm' and that northerners, in turn, *entirely loved and favoured him*; the second Crowland continuator, likewise, was of the firm opinion that Richard gave his greatest confidence to, and placed the greatest reliance on, men from the north of England; and historians, too, have firmly stressed both the importance of Richard's northern background and connections by 1483 and the role of northerners during his protectorate and reign. Certainly, Richard of Gloucester's rule of the north between 1471 and 1483 seems to have been notably successful: his material advancement in the region, both as a result of royal patronage and his own efforts, can be traced in the records; he built up a powerful and loyal affinity there; and there is plenty of evidence that his government of the north won him a considerable degree of popularity. A.J. Pollard, in his definitive 1990 study of *North-Eastern England during the Wars of the Roses*, has demonstrated that, during the 1470s, Richard of Gloucester established a regional hegemony in the north eclipsing even that enjoyed by Warwick the Kingmaker in the 1460s: in the process he re-united northeastern society, created a formidable personal following and brought a degree of stability to the region not seen for years. Moreover, his successful campaigning against the Scots in Edward IV's last years provided the final flourish to the creation of an enviable reputation: indeed, as a reward, a ducal palatinate was set up for him in the north west (comprising not only of Cumberland but also a substantial slice of south-western Scotland providing, as was his declared intention, he conquered it first). Not that his interests were ever exclusively northern. As Constable and Admiral of England he held national briefs; he attended parliamentary sessions in 1472-5, 1478 and 1483; he went on the 1475 expedition to France, accompanied by a very large retinue, and publicly expressed dissatisfaction at the Treaty of Pecquigny which brought it to an inglorious end; and he generally played a high profile role during ceremonial state occasions.

No one will ever know for certain whether Richard of Gloucester set his sights on the throne immediately he heard of Edward IV's sudden death (on 9 April 1483) or if, at first, he merely intended to obtain firm control of his nephew Edward V so as to prevent the Woodvilles seizing power and ensure his own security. Edward IV himself cannot be entirely cleared of blame for what happened after his demise: his son and heir was a minor who had long resided at Ludlow in a Woodville-dominated environment (and the queen and her family, whether popular or not, had legitimate expectations of a prominent role in the new regime); his only surviving brother (who, arguably, had the best claim to be Protector) was an immensely powerful northern lord who (in part as a result of Edward's generous and sustained patronage) packed a good deal of political clout; and there were divisions in the royal court (most notably between the late king's closest and most loyal supporter William, Lord Hastings and the queen's son, Thomas Grey Marquis of Dorset). Certainly, too, there is evidence that Gloucester believed himself to be vulnerable in the political climate occasioned by his brother's premature death, not least on account of his insecure title to so many of his estates: his precarious hold on the northern Neville lands, in particular, may have provided him with a powerful motive for decisive action (a fact graphically brought home to him by the death of George Neville on 4 May 1483, since his right to much of his northern property was now reduced to a mere life interest). Yet it is Gloucester's *behaviour*, whatever his motivations, that dominated the action-packed months April to July 1483.

Even if, as seems likely, the notion of a long-standing feud between Richard of Gloucester and the Woodvilles is no more than the product of hastily concocted propaganda justifying the duke's moves against them, there is no doubt that a massive gulf *did* rapidly open up between Gloucester and the queen's family once Edward IV was no more. There seems little doubt cither that, initially, William, Lord Hastings gave firm backing to Gloucester as the best means of securing Edward V on the throne (as he thought!). Richard of Gloucester, meanwhile, played his own cards with considerable skill, whether from genuine concern to outmanoeuvre the Woodvilles on behalf of his nephew or flagrant dissimulation in his own self-interest: apparently, he despatched letters from the north of England to both queen and council declaring his loyalty to Edward V, presided over a commemoration service for his late brother in York and (in company with many northern nobility and gentry) swore a solemn oath of fealty to the new king, and then marched south with a large retinue (perhaps on the advice of Hastings, who had already persuaded Elizabeth Woodville that her son need only bring a modest escort to London). On 29 April 1483 Gloucester, and his no doubt predominantly northern entourage, arrived at Northampton: there he joined forces with Henry Stafford, Duke of Buckingham (who had his own reasons for disliking the Woodvilles), entertained the queen's brother Anthony, Earl Rivers and her son Sir Richard Grey and, next morning, promptly arrested the pair of them. Proceeding to nearby Stony Stratford, he took possession of his probably indignant royal nephew, arrested his companions (including Sir Thomas Vaughan) and sent them (along with Rivers and Grey) to the northern stronghold of Pontefract. News of her brother-in-law's dramatic initiative soon reached Elizabeth Woodville in London and, no doubt, thoroughly alarmed, she hastily took sanctuary in Westminster Abbey, along with her daughters and younger son Richard of York. With rumour, suspicion and fear rife in the capital, Richard of Gloucester's real intentions probably now became the subject of increasing speculation. Nevertheless, once Gloucester, Buckingham and the young king entered London on 4 May (amidst vigorous propaganda alleging pernicious Woodville conspiracy), a new date in late June was soon set for Edward V's coronation and, on 10 May, Gloucester was formally appointed protector of the realm by the council.

Once firmly established as protector and perhaps, as Mancini suggests, already aiming at 'mastering the throne' itself, Richard of Gloucester lost no time in beginning to exercise the extensive powers of political patronage now at his disposal: John Russell, Bishop of Lincoln, possible author of the Crowland Chronicle, became chancellor, albeit (according to John Rous) 'much against his will'; close associates like John, Lord Howard and Francis, Viscount Lovell received advancement, as did Henry Percy Earl of Northumberland, while Richard made every effort as well to win over as many former household men and servants of Edward IV as he could; and the Duke of Buckingham, no doubt both for services already rendered and as a guarantee of further positive backing in the future, became virtually a viceroy in Wales. By early June 1483 many Londoners, at least, seem to have become convinced that Gloucester was indeed planning to usurp the throne, and moves may also have been afoot by then, probably involving the Woodvilles and perhaps William, Lord Hastings, to counter his ambitions. Certainly, when the Protector wrote to the city of York on 10 June requesting military assistance (and, significantly, elicited a notably positive response a few days later), he cited a Woodville conspiracy to 'murder and utterly destroy' himself and Buckingham as urgent justification. Growing fears in the capital about Gloucester's intentions must have been given a further massive boost by the dramatic events at the Tower of London on 13 June 1483 when the Protector not only rid himself of Hastings (as the man most likely to resist any moves to displace Edward V) but also removed a pair of staunch ecclesiastical loyalists (Thomas Rotherham, Archbishop of York and John Morton Bishop of Ely) from circulation as well. Contemporary and early Tudor sources alike clearly regarded the peremptory arrest and execution of Hastings, portrayed almost invariably as an honourable and upright magnate whose only fault was an unbending commitment to Edward V and his brother, as the ruthless and deliberate act of a man now firmly set on regality for himself. Richard of Gloucester's justification for his behaviour - a rapidly disseminated story alleging the complicity of Hastings in a conspiracy with the Woodvilles to overthrow him - was widely dismissed as malicious propaganda even at the time. Even if Hastings was not nearly so guileless as the Crowland continuator, for one, would have us believe, his remark that Gloucester and Buckingham 'did thereafter whatever they wanted' seems amply borne out by the events of the next few days. Not only was Elizabeth Woodville forcibly persuaded, by a probably very reluctant Cardinal Thomas Bourchier Archbishop of Canterbury, to allow her younger son Richard of York to leave sanctuary (on 16 June) and join his brother in the Tower, but moves were soon instigated too to secure the execution of Rivers, Grey and Vaughan at Pontefract and ensure the imminent presence in London - where, it was reported on 21 June, there 'is much trouble and every man doubts the other' - of more and more provincial partisans of the two dukes. Now the stage was truly set for the process of usurpation proper to begin.

The precise circumstances surrounding Richard of Gloucester's seizure of the throne remain somewhat mysterious. Even more difficult to sort out are the particular arguments put forward to justify his behaviour and their validity (if any). The confusion in the sources, moreover, probably reflects a certain indecision and uncertainty as to the best procedure on the part of Gloucester and Buckingham themselves. On Sunday 22 June, ironically enough the day on which Edward V's coronation should have taken place, sermons were preached at St.Paul's and elsewhere calling into question Edward IV's right to rule (and his son's after him) on the grounds that he (Edward IV) was a bastard and urging the validity of Richard of Gloucester's claim to the throne as Richard of York's only legitimate and rightful successor. These may well have received a notably cool reception, as did a flamboyant speech delivered by Buckingham to leading men of London in the Guildhall on 24 June. Perhaps it was in this speech that the famous story of Edward IV's pre-contracted marriage to Eleanor Butler, invalidating his later marriage to Elizabeth Woodville and bastardizing his children by her, received its first public hearing. Just such a case for the protector's becoming king may well have been advanced in an elaborate petition emanating from an assembly which should have been a parliament and presented to Richard of Gloucester on 26 June: the pre-contract, as well as the invalidity by reason of his father's attainder of any claim by Clarence's son to the succession, certainly formed the mainstay of a later act of parliament (in January 1484) confirming the new king's title (although the balance of likelihood is that the whole story was a fabrication). Responding to the petition (the very production of which may well have reflected fears in London of Gloucester's ruthlessness if checked and the anticipated arrival in the capital of formidable forces from the north and elsewhere), the Protector formally accepted the crown. Richard III may have been convinced, of course, that he was indeed serving the interests of the nation - but such, through the ages, has all too frequently been the politician's justification for arbitrary action.

Once established on the throne, Richard III made hasty preparations for the coronation of himself and his wife Anne, preparations clearly involving a prominent role for his provincial (especially northern) supporters: en route to London, indeed, northerners (notably Sir Richard Ratcliffe) supervised on the king's behalf the elimination of Rivers, Grey and Vaughan at Pontefract, perhaps, as the Crowland continuator remarks, 'without any form of trial'. Early in July Richard himself visited his newly-arrived forces in their camp to the north of the city of London, and they certainly seem to have been powerfully present on the streets of the capital during the magnificent coronation celebrations of 6 July. Soon after this Dominic Mancini left England for France but, already, rumours had reached his ears in London that Edward V was dead. No one will ever know for certain when, or even whether, Richard III had his nephews murdered in the Tower of London. They had certainly disappeared from view by early July 1483 and there seems to have been a still-born plot to liberate them before the month was out: yet, even during Buckingham's rebellion (when producing them could have scotched widespread reports in southern England that they were dead), they remained firmly hidden from view; also, significantly, their mother Elizabeth Woodville ended up supporting a movement designed to put Henry Tudor, Earl of Richmond on the throne (suggesting that, by October 1483, she had given up all hope that her sons were alive). The presumption must be that the Princes in the Tower had, indeed, met a violent end by early October 1483 - an end sanctioned by their uncle as the culminating act of several months spent in a ruthless pursuit of personal power and security.

Richard III's seizure of the throne did not arouse much enthusiasm in London nor, seemingly, in southern England generally, and northerners, notably prominent during the coronation celebrations, soon began to enjoy the fruits of his patronage. So too did close associates and backers such as Henry Stafford, Duke of Buckingham, John Howard, newly created Duke of Norfolk, and Francis, Viscount Lovell. Even many former servants of Edward IV continued to enjoy the king's favour for the time being (although they may simply have been awaiting the opportunity to rise against him). A fortnight after the coronation, Richard embarked on a major progress, no doubt designed both to consolidate his support (especially in the north) and widen the appeal of his new regime: it culminated in a three-and-a-half week visit to the city of York. As the Crowland chronicler recorded, the king was particularly anxious to create a good impression in his crucial northern power-base (where he not only entertained lavishly in York and invested his son Edward as Prince of Wales in the Minster but also granted the city a relief of almost half the taxes it normally paid to the crown). Even so, he may have been unwise to spend so long away from southern England during these crucial early weeks of the reign: certainly, moves against him were soon being mooted in the south and west and, as he at last made his way southwards again, he heard (at Lincoln on 11 October) that rebellion had broken out.

Clearly, this was a rebellion (or, rather, series of rebellions) of major proportions in the southern counties of England, rebellions involving substantial numbers of gentry and showing the extent of resentment and mistrust felt by many towards the new regime (including men who, up to then, had appeared to support it). Part of the explanation, perhaps, lies in already present suspicion of northemers in Richard's household and administration; fears regarding the fate of the Princes in the Tower played a significant role as well; and then, of course, there is also the puzzling behaviour of Henry Stafford, Duke of Buckingham (hitherto Richard's closest and most spectacularly rewarded supporter). Ominously, the exiled Henry Tudor, Earl of Richmond emerged, at the same time, as a potentially serious rival and his marriage to Edward IV's eldest daughter Elizabeth of York was mooted. Although much of the country (particularly the north of England) remained loyal to the king, and the rebellions were poorly coordinated, they were certainly a major threat to Richard III and one to which he responded vigorously: the uprisings either collapsed or were put down and Buckingham, whose desertion obviously shook the king considerably, was peremptorily executed. Yet, given the extent of southern defection and the numbers who now fled the country, he found himself forced more and more thereafter into dependence on his own affinity. This meant, in particular, men from the north ofEngland, and their advancement in the royal household, and plantation not only in southern and western counties but in the midlands as well, is amply demonstrated. And, although the newcomers never formed more than a minority, their pivotal position in the king's regime in 1484/5 cannot seriously be doubted. No wonder the second Crowland continuator wrung his clerical hands in despair and so welcomed the victory of Henry Tudor at Bosworth:

... so many great lords, magnates and commoners, and even three bishops, were attainted [in the parliament of January 1484] that we nowhere read of the like, even under the triumvirate of Octavian, Anthony and Lepidus. What great numbers of estates and inheritances were amassed in the king's treasury in consequence! He distributed all these among his northerners, whom he had planted in every part of his dominions, to the shame of all the southern people, who murmered ceaselessly and longed more each day for the return of their old lords in place of the tyranny of the present ones.

Since he reigned for so short a time, it is difficult either to judge Richard III's potential and qualities as a ruler or draw meaningful conclusions about his government as king; also, what looks like good kingship and firm government may, in reality, be nothing more than Richard trying to widen and deepen the basis of his support. Nevertheless, he does seem to compare not unfavourably with Edward IV and Henry VII (neither of whom, incidentally, would have much of a reputation if they had to be assessed merely on their early years in power). Richard III's only parliament (perhaps with the king's personal encouragement) passed measures clearly benefitting the people; his establishment of the Council of the North, in 1484, proved both popular and enduring; his determination to promote justice and secure law and order is evident from government records; and, although the cost of providing for the defence of the realm eventually compelled him to resort once more to the unpopular financial devices of Edward IV's later years, he did make some effort to improve royal financial administration as well. Even so, with the threat of Henry Tudor looming ever larger in 1484- 5, his reliance on his own affinity (especially northerners) always remained paramount: indeed, his attempt to consolidate his position during the last months (not least his abortive project to marry his niece Elizabeth of York) may, in the end, have proved counter-productive (since it perhaps weakened his northern support and helped determine the outcome of the battle of Bosworth). Certainly, as Rosemary Horrox has emphasised, when he at last faced his rival on the battlefield early on the morning of 22 August 1485, he was backed very largely by the same men who had helped bring him to power two years previously. Many, though by no means all, probably fought for him with vigour (the Stanleys, Henry Percy, Earl of Northumberland and their men being the notable exceptions), but the king's own death (in the midst of the action and, according to the Crowland Chronicle, striving to the end *like a spirited and most courageous prince*) made the fall of the Yorkist dynasty inevitable.

Notes

1. D.Mancini, *The Usurpation of Richard III*, ed.& Trans CAJArmstrong (Oxford,1969,repr, Glos.1984)
2. *The Crowland Chronicle Continutaions, 1459-1486*, Ed.N.Pronay & J.Cox (Glos.,1986)
3. J.Rous, *History of the Kings of England*, in A.Hanham, **Richard III & his Early Historians** (Oxford 1975)
4. *The Great Chronicle of London*, ed.A.H.Thomas & I.D.THornley (London, 1938, repr.Glos.1983)
5. *Three Books of Polydore Vergil's English History*, ed. H.Ellis (Camden Society,1844).
6. Sir Thomas More, *The History of King Richard III*, ed. R.S.Sylvester (Complete Works, Vol. 2, Yale,1963)
7. Edward Hall, *The Union of the Noble Families of Lancaster & York* (1550 edn. repr. Menston, 1970) Holinshed's *Chronicle*, ed. A & J Nicholl (London, 1927) William Shakespeare, *King Richard III*, ed. Anthony Hammond (London 1981)
8. Jeremy Potter, *Good King Richard?* (London, 1983) provides a comprehensive and vigorous survey of Richard III's fluctuating reputation 1483-1983.
9. James Gairdner, *History of the Life and Reign of Richard III* (2nd edn., Cambridge, 1898)
10. A.L.Rowse, *Bosworth Field and the Wars of the Roses* (London, 1966)
11. D.Seward, *Richard III:England's Black Legend*(London,1983)

12. John Rous, *The Rous Roll* (Glos, 1980)
13. Sir G.Buck,*The History of King Richard III*, ed.A.N.Kincaird, (Glos,1982)
14. Horace Walpole,*Historic Doubts on the Life & Reign of Richard III*, ed.PWHammond (Glos.1987)
15. C.A.Halstead,*Richard III* 2 vols.(London 1844, Repr.Glos,1987)
16. Sir Clements R.Markham,*Richard III:His Life & Character* (London, 1906,repr.1973): Philip Lindsay, *King Richard III* (London,1933), Paul Murray Kendall, *Richard the Third* (London,1955)
17. Charles Ross, *Richard III* (London,1981)
18. C.T.Wood *Joan of Arc & Richard III* (Oxford,1988),Ch.8 *The Deposition of Edward V* and Ch.9 *Richard III*: see also Wood's *The Deposition of Edward V*, **Traditio**, Vol.31 (1975) & *Richard III, William Lord Hastings and Friday the Thirteenth in* **Kings & Nobles in the Later Middle Ages**, ed. R.A.Griffiths & J.W.Sherborne (Glos,1986)
19. C.Richmond, *1485 and all that, or what was going on at the Battle of Bosworth?,* in **Richard III:Loyalty, Lordship and Law** Ed. P.W.Hammond (London,1986)
20. Rosemary Horrox, *Richard III:a Study of Service* (Camb.1989)
21. M.Hicks:*Richard III:The Man behind the Myth* (London,1991; see also Hicks's *False Fleeting, Perjur'd Clarence* (Glos. 1980) revisd edn. Headstart History Publ., 1990 & *Richard III as Duke of Gloucester: A Study in Character* (Borthwick paper, 1986)
22. A.J.Pollard, *Richard III and the Princes in the Tower* (Stroud, 1991) see also Pollard's *The Tyranny of Richard III*, Jnl. of Med. Hist., Vol. 3 (1977), & *North-Eastern England during the Wars of the Roses* (Oxford,1990)

BIBLIOGRAPHY

Selections from the main primary sources can be found in P.W and A.F.Sutton, *Richard III:The Road to Bosworth Field* (London, 1985) and K.R.Dockray, *Richard III: A Reader in History* (Gloucester,1988) The most valuable contemporary narratives are Dominic Mancini, *The Usurpation of Richard III,* ed. & Trans. CAJArmstrong (Oxford 1969, repr. Glos, 1984) and *The Crowland Chronicle Continuations, 1459-1486,* ed. N.Pronay & J.Cox (Glos, 1986) The most influential early Tudor narratives have been *Three Books of Polydore Vergil's English History*, ed. H.Ellis (Camden Socm 1844), & ed. Sir Thomas More, *The History of King Richard III*, ed. R.S.Sylvester (Yale, 1963). Valuable surveys of Richard III's personality, life & reign include: Charles Ross, *Richard III* (London 1981) Rosemary Horrox,*Richard III:a study in service*(Camb.,1989);M.Hicks,*Richard III: The man behind the myth* (London 1991) A.J.Pollard: *Richard III & the Princes in the Tower* (Stroud,1991).